A New Color in the Tapestry

e.e. almaguer

AuthorHouse™

1663 Liberty Drive, Suite 200

Bloomington, IN 47403

www.authorhouse.com

Phone: 1-800-839-8640

AuthorHouse™ UK Ltd.

500 Avebury Boulevard

Central Milton Keynes, MK9 2BE

www.authorhouse.co.uk

Phone: 08001974150

ISBN: 1-4259-4672-0 (sc)

First published by AuthorHouse 8/7/2006

Library of Congress Control Number: 2006906780

Printed in the United States of America

Bloomington, Indiana

This book is printed on acid-free paper.

Designed by Somewhereinthewoods Productions

Typeset by DeAnna Rosenbaum

Photographs by Neil Rosenbaum

Author's Photograph by Carolyn Lindaman

Dedication

The force from somewhere in space, which commands you to write, gives you no choice. You take up the pen when you are told and write what is commanded. There is no agony like bearing an untold story. I, too have a story that has yet to be told, but is sometimes hard to tell because of the fear that chases me. It is not just the fear of what I might say, but also the fear that I could tell my story and have it ignored or disrespected. So now I tell some of my story in poetry as that force weaves a new color in the tapestry.

I dedicate this book to my grandchildren and great-grandchildren. For the leading roles of support and encouragement to my staunch friends who were always there when needed, Ellen Emery, Peryl Bringleson, and Marlene Pharr. Here in Mountain View, Mo., to all the new friends, who unknowingly have boosted me to new insights.

 **Penetrating so many secrets,
we cease to believe in the unknowable.
But there it sits, nevertheless,
calmly licking it's chops.
- H.L. Mencken**

Contents

A New Color
in the Tapestry

A Portrait

Silhouetted against the setting sun,
lost in solitude,
no sooner had the memories broke apart,
pieces still flying,
than the cosmos rotated around her,
total recall,
by now her bones dead tired and mauled.

Each ev'ntide she took out the treasure chest
gently caressed each precious gem.
Each had an astounding story to tell her once again.
She lovingly palmed the gem of her first-born
to her breast.

A ghost that haunted her for nigh thirty years,
dances across her vision as prima ballerinas.
In tune to the beat of the ocarina
and the thump of a diverse drum frontier.

A shadow crept like a clinging vine choking
a people with anguish deep in the souls.
Deep crevices in many hearts only time
alone would heal scars and mold.
　　　Maybe never!
But lives excelled for being touched
by one of such a light.

Light breaks where no sun shines,
Where no sea runs, the water of the
heart pushes in their tides,
and broken ghosts with glow-worms
in their heads and things of light,
file through the flesh where no
flesh decks the bones to abide.

I saw the moon and heard her sing,
I heard her sing and saw the moon.

e.e. almaguer 3/23/01

Windswept Tree

I know I hung on that windswept tree,
swung there for many long nights,
wounded by my own blade,
bloodied by booze.
Myself an offering to myself:-
bound to the tree that no woman knows.

None gave me bread,
none gave me drink,
down to the deepest depths I peered
when I found THEM,
with a roaring cry I seized THEM up,
then dizzy and fainting, I fell.

THEY gave me bread, THEY
gave me love, well-being I won and
wisdom, too.
I grew and took joy in my growth —
from a word to a word, I was led to a word,
from a deed
to another deed.

No longer hanging from that windswept
tree,
I now follow a HIGHER POWER'S will.
For through HIS grace, HE gave me the gift
of HIS presence.

Each day I have only to remember -
in the spiritual life,
I am always at the beginning.
Remembering this helps me defeat my
addiction to "GETTING AHEAD."
For when I experience a true present,
that is when everything happens.

e.e. almaguer 5/24/98

A Ship Passing...

In the midst of a dense atmosphere of grief
and lonely mire,
you appeared, to soothe, calm, desire
and inspire.
A vital tantalizing breath of fresh air
you brought,
so young and yet so full of thought.

Dear friend I called you, one of my many
names for you,
you knew what land I was in by the timbre
of my voice.
You banished gray days from musty gloom
to gold,
my heart ran amuck, had no rudder, you stole
my heart,
taught me about service and held me blindfold.

We went then when evenin' was spread out
against the sky,
like a patient etherized upon the table.
Let us go, through certain half-deserted
streets, the muttering retreats,
the hills of primal memory are drained.
And the dim summits of their frosty spars,
whose tops are nibbled by the grazing stars,
thawed by the rising moon of our desire,
and fusing into consciousness and fire.

...in the Night

Down through the sounding of the canyons
of the soul,
their rich alluvium of starlight roll.

Moments of white rapture never die, they
flutter through my memories,
like moon-moths on fragile perfumed wings
glinting with stardust.
I had the time of my life and I never felt
this way before.
A bittersweet gift you bestowed to me,
as you turned and crept to her asea.

I gave you up like a burp, for a better weather
inside my guts,
and yes, I want it all—grab, gaggle, and rut—
as sure as deaths no breather.
Though you wouldn't know, being dead as
yesterdays squall—
where the seas a diamond—spilling toss
in the bright brace of today's air,
to glitter me time and place.
I'm glad I didn't miss the dance
and ran the race.

e.e. almaguer 5/26/01

Dangling Sequined Pumps

I will try to paint you a picture of long,
long ago, of a young lady in her prime.
Who everyone just knew would come
to no good end and not climb.
With fanny perched atop the barstool…
her favored rum and coke in hand,
glug, glug, down the hatch, started the whirlpool.
Ambrosial first long swig caressed her
throat and took command…
purred like a kitten, flooding through all her veins.

She knew it was no-mans land…
a pseudo mask smile and bravado of
    "I don't give a damn!"
Her labyrinth brain coaxing, "It's O.K., it's O.K."
Cross your leg and dangle that sequined spike
heel on the tip of your toe…
You're so sexy and all aglow.

In strutted her drinking buddy, so handsome and fine,
a rum and a coke, a shot and beer, he called
and then we'll dine.
From the amber elixir, she slipped into the shadowed,
shimmering aubergine of beautiful apparitions,
a spectacle so electrifying it held her in it's grip.
Wavering curtains of translucent color that dance
across the heavens, and enthralls with an ethereal light.
Red, yellow, blue, orange and lavender,
she rode the rainbow dangling her sequined spike heel
on high.

Now some years later…no need for rum and coke,
she walks in beauty, poetry in motion.
Her heart a virtual treasure chest, of the ones
who helped along the way.
Many decades she has journeyed this paradise
planet, with many twists and turns in the trail.

Her knarley, time-worn hands told some of the
tale, of each enterprise she undertook and didn't fail.
Her heart code sent the spirit and message ahead,
lay down your tools of war.
Surrender to the God inside to lead,
with Him, she now rides the rainbow of
red, yellow, blue, orange, and lavender,
still dangling her sequined spike heel,
while looking and waving at the sky
fat with moon and stars.

The phoenix consumed itself by fire, later
to rise renewed from its ashes.

e.e. almaguer 8/2/99

My Corner of the World

In the calm of night, journeying
through dreamland,
I became aware of angel kisses
on my cheek.
Next, a buzzing in my ear,
whispering...awake, awake!
Tis' time for the message we bring!!

Heavy-laden with sleep I flounder
and plod my way to the expectant desk.
Meekly lying in wait, my cowardly yellow
palette...
taunting, flaunting, "Who do you think
you are?"
"Ha, Ha, you don't know how to compose!"

BEGONE....BEGONE....
You evil critic, I'll paint
what the Spirit's compass
reveals to me.
Deep into the night at
my trojan desk, my pen
scampers across the page to
excavate my vein of gold.

A sequence of dots and dashes,
spelling depths, crypts,
cross-lights and moon wisps.
A search for syllables to shoot
at the barriers of the unknown
and the unknowable.

A messenger woman performing
her nervous pygmy chores…
drawing lines —
making comparisons…
a world like this, a moon like
that,
the mind like a wire birdcage,
trapping… yet another poem.

e.e. almaguer 7/05

Magic of an Ordinary Day

O'er the horizon bringing a new day of destiny,
crept in the dawn, dew still clinging to each
blade of grass on the lawn.
Off to the sweat shop, tripping down the stairs,
she whistled a merry tune.
With a gasp of surprise, she spied him standing
at the bottom, an ethereal god hewn.
He said, "I've come to milk the cow," with milk bucket
in hand,
"My name is Rudy, and I hear you work with my
brother Louie at his stand.

That ordinary day, in February, nineteen forty-seven,
her world swirled and turned topsy-turvy upside down.
He invited her to a movie that eve and breathily she agreed
to go uptown.
Each eve constant companions, in and out of bars they went,
three months, soft gentle kisses bubbled electric as fine wine
ferments.
And so, the last day of May, they became man and wife,
vowing to always spend the rest of their life.

Some thirty-three years they muddled along,
each becoming strangers, no longer singing the
the same song.
Eons of candle wax of melted dreams, dripping
slowly, and tore asunder the regime.

e.e. almaguer 8/02

My Wee God Box

My wee God box, heart-shaped of
paper-thin wood,
with strokes of colour for solitude.
A dove perched atop the heart,
inside a wee paper with typed
advise to impart.
Revealing to me to only write a
modest petition and put therein,
let go and let God untangle my
woes and let the healing begin!
My wee God box!!

e.e. almaguer 12/01

Milk and Honey

In the land of milk and honey
I slipped and slid into the heights like a bunny.

Here and there burnished a leaf or two,
the heart excited ready to burst
like shards to appease the king.

An element of shard to convulse
first this soul and then to another.
Like a moon that touches first one and then another,
And sails on the sea, broken lines having fun and glee,
insinuatingly look at me.

e.e. almaguer

Mountain View

Nestled in the arms of the Ozarks I found a refuge,
a sleepy hamlet with vibrant sparks.
At the first gesture of morning,
fog enveloped the mountainside,
slipping into the valley grabbing all things
with eely tentacles.

On a rare summery day in March,
while traipsing through the woods,
eavesdropping on the vibrato songs
of the meadowlark.
A breeze whispers through yellow prairie grasses.
In the distance, a northern barrier hawk patrols,
While nearby leopard frogs chortle in a sinkhole pond.

HUSH...listen....
To the quiet of the night,
ghost fiddle whispers of rosin the bow
dancing through the hills.
With varied plucks and tentative bowings,
Then a slow and groping attempt at "Aura Lee."
Next comes the plaintive call of, *"Chicken in the
bread pan picking out dough."*

All the other towns were but stars,
but you are the "Northern Lights"
a bit of heaven here in the Ozarks.

e.e. almaguer 5/04

Hilltop

In the magic moon light, high on the hilltop,
a curly wind swished her skirttail.
Untainted beauty like the dewdrop,
frozen time in deep-rooted travail.

In the magic moonlight, high on the hilltop,
a hand light touched her, and gave a vision so great.
Into another time and place, she did eavesdrop,
Beauty beyond depiction, she could only gaze and elate.

Now she stands in the magic moonlight, on the hilltop,
but never alone.
The hand touches her each minute and leads,
to stay the course.
Though her skirttail gets swished and blown,
no longer a hostage, but transported and freed.

e.e. almaguer 8/26/01

Prairie Fruits

In the stillness of the night, scanning
the prairie, in line of vision,
erect as soldiers standing in harmony.

Sheaves of grain, pregnant and heavy
laden with fruited beards, as prairie
grass ballerinas performed a ballet,
at their feet in spheres.

From out of the distance came music
of ole' hoot owls with their
querulous tunes,
joining in, came the plaintive cries of
the wolf in symphony with the loon

Across the moon, the ole' cacklin' witch
rode her stalk broom, onto the
silver-coloured field.
Whispering to the soldiers, "It won't
be long, it won't be long for the yield."

Dawn arrived, horses and wagons rolled
and men marched with pitchforks,
to harvest for the cold to feed horses
and porks.

On the outer rims nestled farm houses rested
in peace,
Awaiting the onslaught of winter freeze.

e.e. almaguer 5/26/01

Ole' One-way Road

Thanx for the invitation, but...

Always, always, on the road back
to the land of my youth to
visit for B'days, funerals or visits,
on that bumpy one-way road.

But the last time travelin'
that bumpy ole' one-way road
comin' to the home where I now live
the ole-one way road sang to me
no more, no more, travelin' back
to the land of my youth.
That ole' one-way road going there
is closed to me.
I shall always welcome and treasure
any and all visitors who would travel
that ole one-way road to me.

e.e. almaguer 7/05

Spitfire

Spitfire
by name
by action
she became
oldest of
a clan of
twelve
in baseball
she delved.
A tomboy
by nature
by no
means an
amateur
climbed fences
and trees
her world to
finer see.
At fifteen
fled the nest
flew airplanes
on high
to still finer see
the world in
her glory
and oh so free.

e.e. almaguer 5/03

Dances with Turtles

With this palette of words, let me
paint you a canvas of
a flamboyant lady named Jean,
who spied a turtle meandering in
the middle of the street.
She slams on the brakes and pulls to
the side, stepped to the street, huge
floppy hat so wide, grabbed a palm
frond to shoo him out of harms way,
waving it in tempo to a conga beat.

One two, one two three, side step,
One two, one two three, side step.
Like a ballerina dancing on tippy-toes,
first one way, then t'other;
the turtle snapping at her now and then.
She dances with turtles to save yet one more,
and at last guide him to the side of the road.
Looking around to discover an audience of
cars quiet as mice.

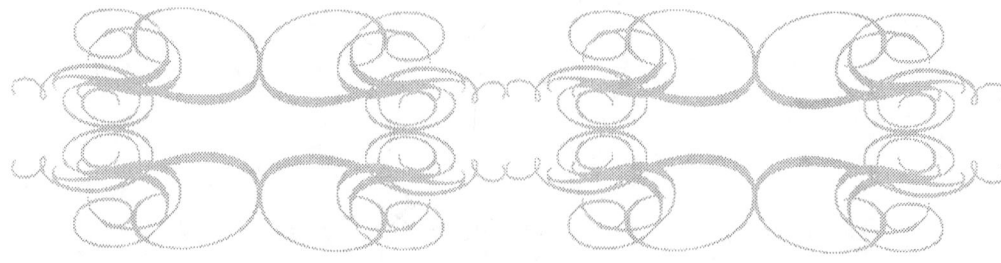

On this day she's so glad she didn't
miss the dance,
she lives her life in growing orbits,
which move out over things of the world.
Perhaps she can never achieve the last,
but that will be her attempt.

She is circling around a Higher Power,
around the ancient tower,
been circling for a thousand years,
and still doesn't know if she is a
turtle, or a storm, or a great song.
BUT SHE DANCES WITH TURTLES!

e.e. almaguer 4/02

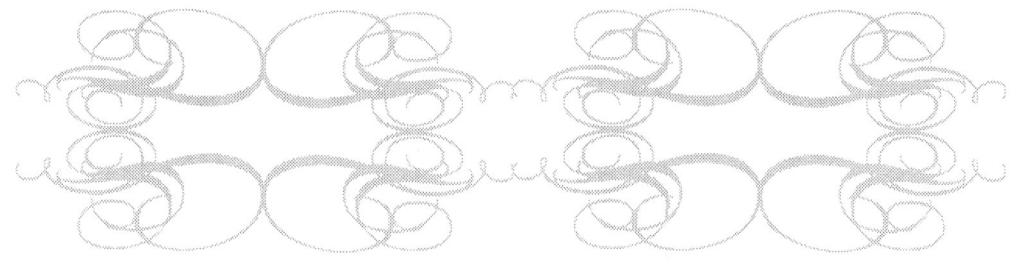

Princess Annie Pananny

Oh the birds and the bees in the cigarette trees
near the soda water fountain,
breezed in Princess Annie Pananny singin',
a song of the land of milk and honey.
On a spring day in the month of April
hiking down a shady lane of sugar
cane and lemonade springs.

A teenager who brought joy and sorrow to
a land that's fair and bright.
A trailblazer that roved the city
at night,
when it was empty, the angels didn't take flight.

At night the bulldogs all have rubber teeth,
And the hens all lay soft-boiled eggs.
The birds and the bees and the cigarette trees,
the lemonade springs where the bluebird sings,
in the Big Rock Candy City!

e.e. almaguer 6/03

Trolley

Clang, clang, clang, went the trolley
ding, ding, ding, went the bell.
Stamp, stamp, stamp in time danced the feet,
ring, ring, ring, nine one one, going to hell.
See, see, saw, Margery Daw.
Blackbird spied his knickers,
and snickered Haw, Haw!!

e.e. almaguer

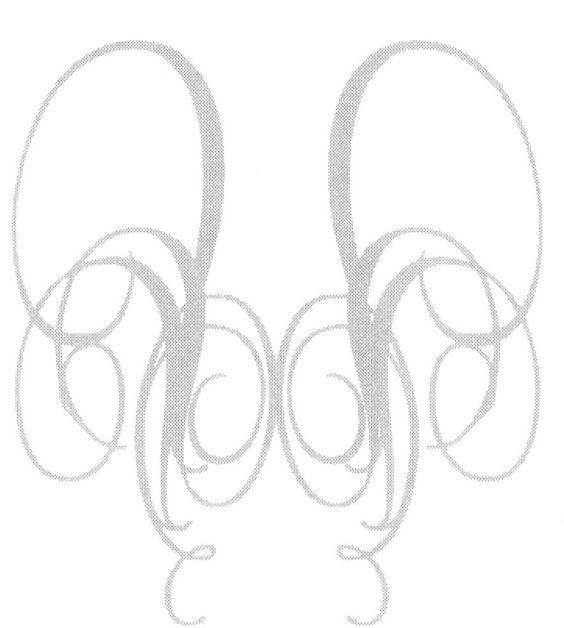

A Gift

A gift more dandy, no one has 'ere been given,
one I would like to share with all who liven.
Here a needle, there a needle, oops one here too,
a smile, an ear, a fellow so true.
Also manipulates errant bones to the place they belong.

Witches Brew

Bubble, bubble, toil and trouble,
begone and zap her no longer rubble.
Frog legs, spiders, and herbs boiled, too,
take with brew, a bewitching smile remedy
and no more blues.
Always a smile and a helping hand,
he's the bestest in the land.
DOC PETERSON!!

e.e. almaguer 2/03

Terminator Twins

Dynamic Duo

Just two of the names they were called…
as they twisted and turned my body parts,
into a pretzel 'till my muscles did scald,
they called it therapy, I called it tortured arts.

Mike and Justin, Justin and Mike smiled ever
so sweetly,
invited me in to their dungeon of torture,
come…my lovelies and we'll make you
new athletically,
it's for sure we're no amateurs.

Now don't get me wrong and
lose your head,
their tenacity and pluck has kept me
from the cane or the invalid bed.

Sooo…without further adieu…
for all the knotted and scalded muscles,
to you I tip my hat and you can drink the brew!

GRACIAS!!

e.e. almaguer 6/00

Three Illinois Grande Dames

Three scintillating grande dames from Illinois,
jamin' and jivin', sailing to St. Crioux.
An artist, an interior designer, and one a poet,
wearing with honor on each shoulder her artist epaulet.

In the great state of Florida, they were destined to meet,
at a book signing in Vero Beach they did greet.
Lunched by the beach, chattering a mile a minute,
sharing and giggling for all was in it.

Entered another grande dame from Baltimore,
who in her clan is no sagamore.
In harmony we all became "The Four Grande Dames,"
To the end jamin' and jivin' our claim to fame.

e.e. almaguer 9/02

A Blithe Pixie Sprite

Taunting, catch me if you can, with peals of laughter,
ballerina words pirouetted across my screen of vision.
Hurry, hurry, before the choicest elude you, as vixen,
imp, siren, champion, flaxen, etc. scrolls across the screen.

Flaxen hair, quite outspoken, and mysterious smile,
copying the proverbial cat who ate the canary.

She has entered the realm of my friend,
where my soul can be naked and
she asks nothing of me but to be myself.

In an instant, turn around…
the melancholy touches deep,
inside her where no one can reach,
and she dances on the edge of the wind.

An author of women's world,
championing women to discard the
pseudo-masks,
shaking the shards of that glass ceiling from her hair.

for Marlene

e.e. almaguer 8/02

Wilted Wildwood Rose

An orphaned wilted wildwood rose,
lost in a sea of wildwood roses.
Perky and bright ones shunning her,
waving in the breeze in a blur.

Her wilted head brushes the ground,
turned to the green thumbs, pleading
for help to be sound.
They mentored out plant food
day by day,
lent a hand to hold up her
head to stay.
Bloom where you're planted
they did relay.

This wildwood rose came to know
the kernel of her authentic truth.
More upright each passing day,
slowly, one petal at a time
unfolds virelay.
Wilted wildwood rose sprouting to
full bloom and youth.

I have a bouquet of friends,
but you are my wildwood rose.
for Ellen Emery

e.e. almaguer 8/02

Ole' Punk'in Tomcat

My ole' tomcat in the truest sense, gadded all night
and slept all day hence.
Sitting asleep like a carving in space.
his eyes of ebony,
closing into slit, when peril
threatened his home base.

Pun'kin hid in his fur-light, all humped up,
higher and higher.
At a moments notice, would pounce and make love
in his purr-song around my legs with might.

His Majesty, a second name, his looks seemed to speak,
almost clear and sometimes hazy as dreg.
He would crawl in my lap, curled like a ball of yarn,
rev up his motor, content as the flowing Marne.

e.e. almaguer 8/02

Stormin' Norman & Pooch

Stormin' Norman, Stormin' Norman,
Where oh where have you been, Stormin' Norman?
Why I've been to run my traps and
check the field mice.
I'm just a roamin' hobo and cannot
leave this way of life.

I'm Lord of the mansion, a sleek Siamese,
who rules the kingdom by stealing hearts,
a favor now and then by stroking your legs.
But I'm just a roamin' hobo and cannot
leave this way of life.

Dolly dog, Dolly dog……
Where have you been, my darlin' Dolly dog,
Why I've been seein' over the home fires,
I'm a pointer and cannot leave my mistress.

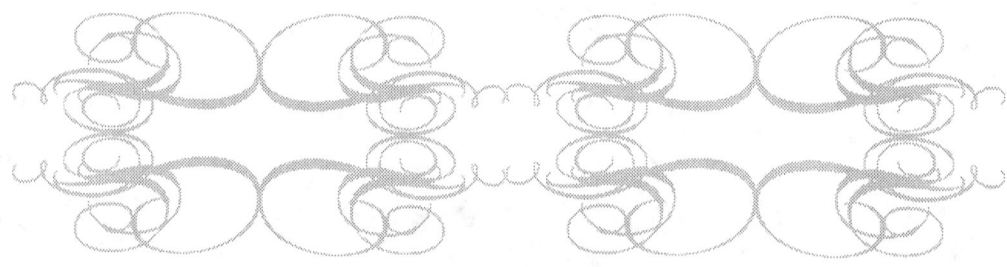

Ole' butterscotch nose patrols the yard,
Keepin' an eagle eye on the quarry.
Queenly in nature, robber of hearts
and settees.
Hugs and unconditional love for all and
To the Lindaman family riches of mirth.

Now and then you can spy them on their
heavenly rounds,
Stormin' Norman and Miss Dolly sparklin'
up the heavens, for one and all.

e.e. almaguer 12/03

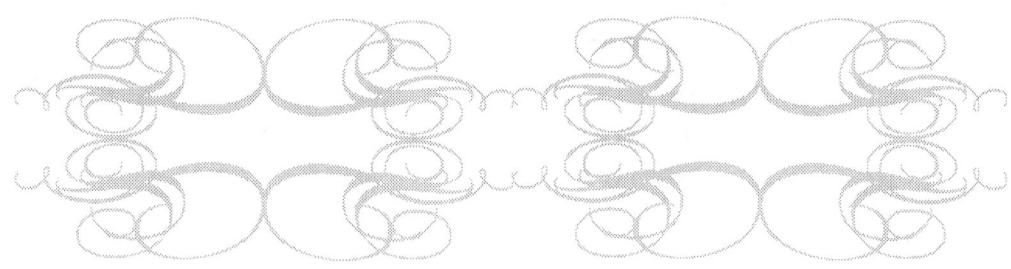

Barb-wire Escapade

When I was five or thereabouts...
well nigh onto to supper-time and
I in a pout.
from the kitchen Mama chanted in her
sing-song voice...shh
listen...listen...hear the old Model T
chuggin' for all it's worth,
daddy's comin' down the lane.

High-tailin' out of the house yelling
"Daddy, Daddy."
Mama callin' a warnin',"Don't climb
the barb-wire fence, my
sweet Missy!"

So excited was I to see my Daddy...
climbed the fence to yet farther see...
Half-way up, my bare-foot slipped
faster than greased-lightnin'
the barb-wire seized my left cheek,
tearing a gash to the side of my mouth.

Strong arms lifted and cradled me,
my Daddy whispering, "You're alright
I've got you."
While on deer feet he beat a path to our house.

My daddy cradled me while I hiccuped
and sobbed,
as Mama cleansed and kissed, bandaged and
kissed the pain away,
as her cool hands swabbed.

Now today I wear it…
as a dimple beauty mark and
                even after all these years…
can still hear my Mama's
warning and loving touch,
and feel the tender cradled strength of
Daddy's sheltering arms.

e.e. almaguer 4/17/06

Sleepwalker at Five

I rise slowly from my tangled bed and
shuffle outside.
Sensing only the pale humidity of
the night,
the grass cool and wet on my bare feet.

Hello Darkness, my old friend,
I've come to talk to you again.
With loyal buddy Spot trailing behind,
I search for the moon to unwind.
Then, see what looks like the China Clipper.

We shuffle to the open well to
see our reflections,
Spot sees us and barks in suspicion.
Mom hears Spot and rushes to see the matter,
her daughter, sleepwalking like
an acrobater.
Her soothing voice and gentle hand,
lead me to bed to dream
of the Starship Command.

e.e. almaguer 4/06/04

Talk to Me

Talk to me…
speak my name,
on a lofty mountain tree..
sat an owl with no name.

Talk to me…
speak my name,
sat his mate with three..
babies whom he did claim.

Talk to me…
speak my name,
so they wouldn't be the same..
he called them Lea, Bea and Cree.

Talk to me...
speak my name,
owl with no name, spoke he..
who, who, Dad is my name.

e.e. almaguer 3/97

Dreamin, Dreamin, Dreamin

The nighttime falls so…
deep, deep, deep.
It's now time for…
sleep, sleep, sleep.
And visions of angels do…
creep, creep, creep.
Singing lullabies for the soul to…
keep, keep, keep.
Where little Ellie does play and…
leap, leap, leap.
Angels give strength for her to…
reap, reap, reap.

e.e. almaguer 6/05

Because of You

With hands of silk,
velvet, purring words,
pollinating fingers soothing
my head and tears.

With crow's feet astride
dancing blue eyes.

Frenetic drumbeats of
our hearts.....
each day, all holidays,
spiraled into one.

No human language required to
chart the emotional
weather of our souls.

Walking along a
barbwire fence,
bend low again...
night of summer stars.
Each caress will last
forever...

He is gone!

e.e. almaguer 10/05

A Touch of Class

Please note how much you are
applauded and cherished,
for you, nothing but the best is wished.
You all made me look mighty good,
and stole my heart like Robin Hood.

Some come into our lives and soon
disappear,
some come to move our souls to dance.
They awaken us to new understanding
with the passing whisper of wisdom.
Some make the sky more beautiful to gaze upon.
They stay in our lives for awhile, leave
imprints on our hearts, and we are never
ever the same.

Now at the end of trusted servant bliss,
I shall miss you all, but leave you with
a stolen kiss...

dedicated to the volunteers of St. Lucie county

e.e. almaguer

Ode for Jim E.

Umber waves of sand sift softly across your grave,
and winds frolicked down the mountains to the desert floor.
James E. Fisher Jr. etched in granite forever brave,
where they lodged your ashes, you took a detour.
Now you ride the breezes and caress my cheek.

My whole heart rises up to bless,
your name in pride and thankfulness,
your leave for one more ride with me.
You stood on the heights of life with
a glimpse of a height that was higher.
What sight so lured you through the fields you knew,
as where earth green stole into heavens own hue?

A flowery tale more sweetly than our rhyme:
what leaf-fringed legend haunts about thy shape
of deities or mortals, or of both,
in Tempe or the dales of Arcady?
Heard melodies are sweet, but those unheard
are sweeter; therefore, ye soft pipes, play on;
not to the sensual ear, but, more endeared,
pipe to the spirit ditties of no tone.

By sweet enforcement and remembrance dear,
and pardon that thy secrets should be sung
even into thine own soft-conched ear.
What are this world's true joys-ere the great voice,
From it's fair face, shall bid our spirits fly.

e.e. almaguer 9/03

Baby's Breath

Baby's breath:-
Lay a whisper on my pillow.

Baby's arms:-
Leave the winters on the ground.

Baby's cooing:-
Greet the robins in the willow.

Baby's feet:-
Imprint my heart spellbound.

Baby's eyes:-
Flood our darkness with laughter and dance.

Baby's toes:-
This little piggy went to market,
This little piggy stayed home.

Baby's lashes:-
Gives angel kisses leaving all in a trance.

Baby's smile:-
Cloud mover and path lighter, no more to roam.

Baby's smell:-
To treasure your essence and peach soft skin.

Baby's grown-up:-
I wake up lonely, despair of silence,
But I'm sheltered by your heart.

e.e.almaguer 9/03

An Angel in Disguise

Mother Teresa

Take notice as the brush strokes of words
swoop across the paper canvas, begging
chose me, chose me,
singing like humming birds,
into the stratus like an angelus.

You can tell by the tilt of her head
and a half-smile…
still waters run deep with steel threads
in a soft pulse.
You can tell her temperature by the look
on her face,
like Eleanor Roosevelt had when she came up
out of the coal mines.
Hovering on the edge just waiting to help,
greets and makes you feel welcome.
Sees a need and pitches in, all
the while keeps things running smoothly.

If…she should cast the gift of a
thought into the heart of a friend, a kindness
that is as giving as the angels give.
Her life lightly dances on the edges of time
like dew on the tip of a leaf.
Her lantern heart, a spiritual D.N.A.

for Rhoda
e.e. almaguer 5/02

An Old Young Man

I spied a young man by the side of the road,
holding a sign, "will work for food."
He coulda' been an uncle, husband or son
with no abode.
A bushy, scruffy beard, he'd been outa'
livelihood.

I rode on by and when almost home,
A nigglin' at the nape of my neck said
go back.
buy some food for this man who roams,
off to Wendy's drive-in, order food to fill up the sack.

In haste I returned, to see if he still sat there,
Oh good, yes he was, "HEY MISTER," I called.
Pushed the sack to him and said, hope it fills you
to the brim.
I know it's not much but hope it sets your heart astir.

Waved goodbye and my heart felt like dancing
and hoped,
That maybe, just maybe, that young old man
might someday,
become an old, old man.

e.e. almaguer 6/02

Celebrated Life-giver

Frances Ford Fisher 1910-2004

At the first gesture of morn, dear
Mom, you come bathing my spirit
in a new delight.
In each child you bore,
your flower blooms again
and again.

At evn'tide, if I may guess,
thy beauty wears
a smile of such delight.
As brilliant and bright to
touch us who reign here.

I know you've set the stage
for bingo,
where you're traipsing in that
great beyond,
and winning your share as
you did here…
where, when you skated on thin ice,
you learned to dance.

But even a mom sometimes
needs a comforting pillow on
which to lay her head.

When I awaken in the mornin'
hush and feel the swift uplifting
rush of quiet birds in circled
flight,
I will know it is you.

Mom, remember when I told
you…
you'll probably die before me
and if you do….
Do you see that big old star up
there in the heavens called
Venus?
Would you wait there for me, so
I'll know where to find you.

So now the colour has gone home
in to the eyes,
and the lights that shone are shut
again.
and that no-place which gave birth,
shall close,
The rainbow and the rose.

e.e. almaguer 3/11/06

Life

Black Granite Wall

Can't you feel the breath
of all the soldiers living and dead?
For pray tell, some of the living are in death,
as surely as their life blood was drained and bled.

Do you not see the vacant stares?
The spirit sucked from their life force.
Do you ask about them and their heirs,
Can't you feel the heavy remorse?

Can you feel the spirit
of loved ones living and dead?
Some cut down early in life,
now exquisite,
others left to carry on like thoroughbreds.

Touch it, touch it, the thready pulse of many,
olympian raspy sighs, ragged sobs, broken hearts,
sweet revenge,
blood-red gaping wounds crusted over, in painful agony.
Touch it, touch it, no longer a need to avenge.

A young son, daughter, dad, or mom, a conscript,
bloodied by battle of war and life, but no more.
In dark reaches of night, they march past my memory
door on the flagship,
a symphony of voices, of our loved ones we
cannot ignore.

They stand on the cusp waiting for us,
melodious symphony singing, with angels we spoke.
Gallivanting and free as the Pegasus,
we long for the day to see our gentlefolk.

Can you feel the breath?
Can you feel the pain?
Can you hear when it speaks?
Can you feel the touch?
Can you see it all?
Can you hear the secrets?
Can you feel the cleansing?
It shares the pillow to the future!
FEEL, TOUCH, SEE, HEAR, the flame of the Spirit,
emanating from
the BLACK GRANITE VIETNAM WALL.

for P.F.C. Benjamin Almaguer,
killed 3/10/68 in Vietnam

e.e. almaguer 4/23/98
his mother

Black Granite Wall

Forever Young

It was the worst of days, it was March 10, 1968.
From the steamy quagmire jungles of Vietnam,
on patrol, this teen of ours
snuffed out by friendly fire
sent home from across the seas,
wrapped in his coffin cocoon.
He would be forever young!

It was the worst of days, it was March 20, 1968.
The ides of March winds blew
bringing three inches of snow.
Arctic and wet with no place to go-but,
lacing and icing around each heart so slow.
He would be forever young!

Like soldiers marching in parade,
the cars escorted him to his final resting place.
Hands lovingly touched the casket in
final tribute,
a rose so tenderly placed along with a tear,
gently they lowered him in the sod,
plop, plop, sounded clods of dirt
being dropped.
He would be forever young!

The sharp crack of guns fired and acrid smell
of belching gun smoke in final salute,

while the air thickly vibrated with
ghostly cries of TAPS
echoing into the very fiber of mourners.
He would be forever young!

Nigh on to winter on his day of birth,
a family pilgrimage to his last place of sleep.
They came bearing a cake of white
daisy frosting and red rose buds candles.
He would be forever young!

The pink nipples of the earth in springtime,
the long eyelashes of summer's look,
the harvest laughter of tawny autumn,
the winter silence of land in snow covers.
He would be forever young!

Long shadows of Vietnam spread over all
and the great price be paid,
and the home be empty,
and the family wishing,
under the chimneys of winter-time,
children of the world shall sing new songs.
He shall be forever young!

e.e. almaguer 10/29/92

The Heart of Christmas

The heart of Christmas…
does not come in a little gift bag,
it does not come with a gift tag.
It does not come with a million dollars,
or with people in stiff white collars.
It does not come with a pretty bow,
it does not come during a big Broadway show.

The heart of Christmas…
has an ear to hear the silent cry of a child,
to feed and cuddle him with love beguile.

The heart of Christmas…
is a genuine friend who sticks by your side,
declaring, oh what fun at yuletide!
and when sick, brings chicken noodle soup,
even knowing you have the "creepin' croup."

The heart of Christmas…
is the love of a soulmate,
with a twinkle in their eyes, incarnate.
The smell of a rose or the snow of winter,
to look at the creation of a majestic Dinter,
from whom comes all Peace and Serenity.

The heart of Christmas…
comes with dancing kaleidoscope festival lights,
pushing out the darkness with delight,
celebrating all family, friends, and neighbors with a bite.
Incandescent hearts pulsating love,
all from that long-ago "DOVE."

'Tis the Gift it 'tis…
"The Heart of Christmas"…

e.e. almaguer 11/04

One More Christmas

One more Christmas,
all alone she rocks,
listening, for a key in the lock.

One more Christmas,
all alone she sees their faces,
and remembers their baby graces.

One more Christmas,
all alone in the morning hush,
she hears the thrill of their voices gush.

One more Christmas,
all alone she delves,
Christmas' past, she must shelve.

One more Christmas…
Maybe, just maybe, the phone will ring,
and a familiar voice will sing…
Merry Christmas, Mom, I love you!

One more Christmas……

e.e. almaguer 9/04

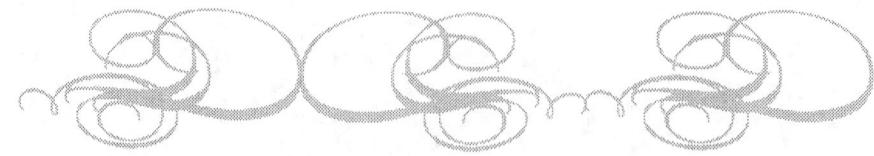

Christmas Tree Skirt

O' Christmas tree skirt,
O' Christmas tree skirt,
how lovely you look with
poinsettias so pert…

in each and every stitch
you'll find…
a wealth of love, prayers
and serenity…
blended together to bind…

each poinsettia holds it's tiny
light…
that makes this gift to
sparkle bright…

Fly, fly across the many
miles…
and land in grandiose style…

O' Christmas tree skirt!

e.e. almaguer 12/15/04

Lament

You were my landscape, the mountains,
the sky, the valley where I planned orchards
by and by.
I did not suspect the lava simmering beneath
the slope.
I did not detect the tremor mounting like a
bomb ticking into a new birth.

You were my green earth when the mountain
came apart in pieces.
It's farthest reaches eclipsing the sun.
I still was not certain what had been done.

You were my landscape…what I took
for granted—
all that has been slanted skyward,
falling to earth, ashes, debris and heat,
shattered glass, broken boards and dirt,
for what it's worth,
I LOVED YOU!!

e.e. almaguer 5/02

Assassination

I waited for you to make the sun rise,
to make our house a home…
while waiting lost my integrity…and
myself.
I waited for you to make a soft place to fall,
to conquer wind, rain, lightning, and still
the waters.
I waited for you to shelter me with
your love…
and you couldn't, wouldn't or didn't
know how.

What deep wounds ever closed with-
out a scar?
The heart's bled longest, and but
heal to wear
that which disfigures it; and
they who war.

My lamp must be replenished,
but even then…
it will not burn so long as I watch,
that which I lov'd and long must love,
like common earth must rot.

e.e. almaguer 7/05

He's Just an Old Alky

He turned sixty-five last Sunday,
his dirt-cheap booze turned flat and
he don't know what to do.
He gets out there in the twilight zone
where it don't make any sense.
Should he hang on to the old…
or grab on to the new?

He was sure, back in the young years,
when he was master of it all.
He ain't tryin' to change nobody,
he's just tryin' real hard to not fall.
Should he hang on to the old…
or should he grab on to the new?

Through the blurry booze fog,
he still dream'in of Woodstock.
He still ain't changed his lifestyle,
cause he likes it thata way.
Should he hang on to the old
or should he grab on to the new?

He's just an old alky…
pulled one way the t'other…
should he hang on to the old
or should he grab on to the new?

e.e. almaguer 5/04

High Tide

High tide of
guilt…
crashed his
brain.

High tide of
guilt…
pouncing over
and over…
th-rum, th-
rum,
against his
brain.

Each ebb to
the sea…
netting bits
of
brain…
matter to the
oozy bottom.

e.e. almaguer 5/05